More praise for *Alien Miss*

"In this reckoning of what it means to be seen as 'alien,' as Other, Duan constellates inter-generational ache. *Alien Miss* sings forth an anthem of resistance and resilience. Especially as a Chinese American poet too, the 'yolky stars' of each poem oozed straight into my ghostly guts. I am so grateful for this book, this poet."
—Jane Wong, author of *Overpour*

"Duan wields her craft with keen intellect and infinite generosity in this ambitious collection that tenderly ushers into existence a glorious host of voices. Hailing the collective grit that undergirds racialized womanhood in America, her poetry becomes a radical invitation to celebrate clear-eyed and unflinching joy."
—Jasmine An, author of *Naming the No Name Woman*

WISCONSIN POETRY SERIES

Edited by Ronald Wallace and Sean Bishop

ALIEN
MISS

CARLINA DUAN

The University of Wisconsin Press

Publication of this book has been made possible, in part, through support from the Brittingham Trust.

The University of Wisconsin Press
728 State Street, Suite 443
Madison, Wisconsin 53706
uwpress.wisc.edu

Gray's Inn House, 127 Clerkenwell Road
London EC1R 5DB, United Kingdom
eurospanbookstore.com

Printed in the United States of America
This book may be available in a digital edition.

Library of Congress Cataloging-in-Publication Data

Names: Duan, Carlina, author.
Title: Alien Miss / Carlina Duan.
Other titles: Wisconsin poetry series.
Description: Madison, Wisconsin : The University of Wisconsin Press, [2021]
    | Series: Wisconsin poetry series
Identifiers: LCCN 2020035236 | ISBN 9780299331344 (paperback)
Subjects: LCGFT: Poetry.
Classification: LCC PS3604.U236 A68 2021 | DDC 811/.6—dc23
LC record available at https://lccn.loc.gov/2020035236

For my sister,
who makes me possible

The land of the living was not that far removed from the domain of the ancestors.
There was a coming and going between them . . .
—CHINUA ACHEBE

CONTENTS

INHERIT WHAT YOU CAN

ALIEN MISS

Is there only one source? You have sources of sources—sources of tributaries.
—LORINE NIEDECKER

ALIEN MISS

in the mirror she swiped paw across mouth, leaked open.
roman alphabet, eel-like, pink, slid inside the body's wet well.

words like *swallow. wallow, wail, rinse.* she practiced curving each
w between the lips, letting the diphthongs roll out. each syllable welled

into a small coin tucked into gums. if she spoke the words right,
the bus deposited her body at the proper street. spoke the words well

and she'd get the fattest fish at the supermarket, the one the big man
beckoned to with his big wrist. *wild, while. quiet.* spoke the words like a *well-*

educated miss, he said, *oriental miss, butterfly miss, miss, you look like you're not
from here. chink, chin*—miss in the mirror tearing apart her jaw, a well-

oiled machine. miss in the mirror turning her head this way, then that,
tilting it against the light. miss unzipping her dress to reveal a stairwell

full of translucent birds. tongue like a serpent's, coiled
and forked at the tip. she hissed and let it all fly out, a swell

of noises that made the buses puff black clouds of gas, made peaches
crumple into soft, nude skins. *slant-eye miss! dangerous miss!* a tongue well

behaved until it disintegrated. *nǐ zhī dào wǒ shì shéi ma?* she asked to
nobody, the air around her heaving with animals, with dust. *well?*

in the mirror she held up her hands and examined them for traces
of pollution, stars. *do you know who I am?* she asked to nobody, well

adjusted, by now, to the silence furring her breasts; the silence, a pelt
atop her skull. *alien miss. speak* ENGLISH*, miss*, her tongue dwelled

inside a flailing mouth. in the mirror she swiped paw across face, leaked
until her body, a faucet, beckoned the words out. *wǒ zǒu le!* farewell, farewell.

ALIEN MISS READS SECTION 14

That hereafter no State court or court of the United States shall admit Chinese to citizenship; and all laws in conflict with this act are hereby repealed. (1882)

then it was time to go to work. the laboratory lay with its

innards spilled open: beakers and microscopes, fish skin

stretched taut, then mounted onto slides. stray hairs on

tiles, as thin as matchsticks, stiff beneath her boots.

in another year—not hers—fields yawned wide.

men riding boats came, in hoards, with their

hands in their pockets, docking their mouths on hard

crusts of bread. a string of questions cast their bodies

to tighter nets, crisscrossed and dented at the skins:

how many stairs alight the case in your sister's house?

what are the locations of moles on your sister's body?

when did you receive your gold tooth?

shame wept inside a salty mouth. answerless,

they cocked their thumbs to the dirt.

in her year, she tapped her thumb against

the glass. gills and scales. men and their

calves, beating against a barrack bed. *home, home.*

want to go home. she placed an eye through

the microscope to look at the specimen: scales,

omega, silver, fat. a slow ghost crawling past:

those men in their boats—*China, California*—only

to be sent back. the mole above her lip glinted.

her body pressed its meat against the lens.

if she looked hard enough, could she

see them there? tiny men sailing a gilded strip

of fish skin, waving their oars, *remember me,*

remember me, begging her for a piece of land?

ALIEN MISS AT THE IMMIGRATION STATION

after A. Van Jordan

IN *[prep.]*

1. *expressing the situation of something that is or appears to be surrounded by something else*:

living *in* the barracks she dreamed nightly of snapping garden vines, gathering eggplants shiny as beetles; a little palm sugar, a little oil, she slithered *in* a pan—crackle-splat, purple drizzle, rounds of eggplants browning *in* fire & oil; fat & lusty grease-filled moons. *in* the barracks she was a daughter and a terror; *in* a square room, she was left to rot. she watched the days go click, click, click, the door shut, the air stale from other hissing breaths; breathe *in* the cots, cages, gruel they fed her *in* chunks, brewed *in* a washtub and piled atop plates . . . do not think of her *in* here; think of her *in* harvest, long summers before the boat, before English crushed like tinfoil against her tongue; eggplants rising *in* slender purple stalks *in* the hushed field *in* the summer after rain, tiny grasses sprung out of a river, think of her *in* the house she ate pork floss *in*, fine and hungry and full of salt, the crops growing, the green roasting, her mother calling her name—

2. *expressing a period of time during which an event takes place or a situation remains the case*:

in 1882, "the coming of Chinese laborers to the United States . . . is hereby, suspended," papers cast alive by Congress, wet with signatures, stamps; *in* small decades, they were laborers, brides; they arrived *in* 1910 by ship, heavy and swollen from the sea; at the Angel Island Immigration Station their bodies levitated *in* minutes, ticking, ticking, alive, alive; forgo mercy and forgo hunger; slurp the pig slop; their muscles *in* 1911, 1912, they turned ghost and ghost again, thought they would die *in* a month, a year; land-starved, starry with sweat, "That the words 'Chinese laborers,' whenever used in this act," should rattle like pork bones in a tin. they worked, they worked, they sing:

3. *expressing a state or condition*:

she was *in* love. she was *in* pain. a woman *in* her state needs nutrition, needs soil for her feet. a woman *in* her state needs a country. aisles. alleyways to roam. *in* her stillness she dreamed of throttling an orange—throwing her nails into the rind, digging 'til she felt the crush, juice splitting against her fist while she dug the seeds out, emptied the gut. at the station, she was *in* a feral state. they called her in for questioning. across the table, she sat. a creature made of acid, sugar, snout, blood.

ALIEN MISS CONSULTS HER PAST

on Angel Island, she finds:

a bolt of blue linen cloth. moles on the chest.
boats, men who boarded them. bound for
a *golden country*. to pave, to stave off
hunger. labor. what's an American dream but
a debt. a price to pay. how to say. *longing,
longing, O say
can you see?* vowels, opened. bare feet
hitting the grass. long sprawls
of land. touching foot to ground. foot
to hardwood floor. water then water
then more water. slats of light
against a long wall. saying her own name
to a room. holding a pool of water
on the tongue.
                    saying her own
name to a tree. to another head, its river of
hair matted on the pillow. barred from
entry. barred from country. barred
while carrying a chain-link fence.
lawful   feral   fearful

  what's in
  the past is in
  the past is in
  the past:

> *That these threats and intimidations and riotous bloody
> acts, in this nation which claims to be a leading nation
> in intelligence, morality, and culture, shock our sense
> of national pride—*

the past is in the future   the future
in a woman who strips down before
crawling into a barrack's lonely
bed. above her, the cloth hangs
to dry. goosebumps on the skin.
practices saying the words
out loud. *by the dawn's early light.*
what so proudly we hailed. what
so proudly we hailed. what so proudly
so proudly,   so
     so

        —O.

ALIEN MISS CONSULTS HER FUTURE

tall windows. brown spiders with marble-sized
bellies, lumbering in after a cool rain. whipping cream
in a roselike puddle atop the kitchen counter. four children,
or perhaps   no children at all. breath. breath. rose
gardens. a house key, hidden beneath the Welcome mat
in a dirty garage. flipping a coin, selecting *heads*.
the wind pushing past automated doors.
on the radio, a disembodied voice, wailing
Resident aliens . . . the green shutters of a Midwestern
house—   no. flipping a coin, selecting
the metal staircase of a fire escape midsummer, perched
above bedrooms of fluorescent light. her mouth
sucking   a cigarette. a cloud
licking a skyscraper. an old woman selling
churros near the train. the groins of the city, or:
another listless day.   a hopeless wallet.
a man yelling *Shut, shut the fuck up*—   a woman
not abiding.   reading Walt Whitman
in a community garden, *Do I contradict myself?*
purple flowers, black mud. *I am large, I contain*—
an iPhone unsilenced.   a coin etched with
wings. spam calls that begin with a robotic voice:
Dear Citizen. parting the black hair straight down
the middle, in an effort to appear more

obedient / unfazed / allegiant / good girl / clean.

buying in. reciting slogans between her teeth.
I pledge allegiance to   Crest in cardboard
boxes. Estée Lauder skin creams. Subway sandwiches
lined with fake pink meat.   in this country, money
can buy   *suspicious activity.*   wet dreams.

11

hardwood floors   or a dozen lemons.   Philadelphia
Cream Cheese. in this country, work hard. receive
statistics.   *pigeons.*   *nobody's* American dream.

alien miss consults her future and reconsiders.
holds the coin flat in her palm. the bald eagle
winks. the silvered head stares past her,
vacant and unconvinced.   in her future,
a phone buzzes.   a cricket chirps. somewhere,
a pool flashes with blue. somewhere,
a nation sends its aliens back—   no.
she does not choose that life, but another.

ALIEN MISS CONFRONTS THE AUTHOR

in the Pacific Northwest, I take my credit card to the over-
priced history museum & melt into the land. green grass, fine
grass, grass growing in the crevices of walls & trees. to be
here. to be far away from every body I was. the curtains sheer
& milky, light tumbling through the windows. my fingers
rubbing blueberries, crushing them to dark constellations
I cast away in fists.   thinking, today, of shears. of my
body. back *there*.   the blue-blue. the blue-hue. blue history
of people I won't belong to but still—I browse through
archives full of men and women with long black hair,
throwing themselves into the land. thread of grass. thread
of immaculate touch.   paper son, or paper
daughter. my own papers marked with wings, the pointed
tip of an eagle's beak.   here, who's made prey?

I pledge allegiance.   to history, who eats me.
to the map, which points to my tongue, soft
and slack   preventing me from uttering   the words:

> The community remains historically a socially
> bifurcated society, divided between the foreign-born
> and the American-born.

O say can you see. by the dawn's early-early.
this morning, in my country, it glowed.

I read the placards: *The railroads provided
especially important benefits for the Chinese
in the American West.* I read, try to muster
up how it was back then: weeds poking

through a chain-link fence—   a tin can full
of cucumbers—   a dog's tongue, salivating—

I putter out.   my throat pushes one word, slick, through
                the crevice of the mouth.

            No.

        in this tongue
        I am resident alien
        made complacent
        by what I'm supposed
        to say: CHINESE
        AMERICAN

        PORCELAIN   RAILROAD GOLD RUSH

        MINING   MINER   "MINE"

                        RICE SPOONED INTO
                        THE BELLIES OF BOWLS

I bash the pictures in half,
crack captions between jaws.

in the museum, the signs wink. I bray.

                        ∼

Why are you even interested
in writing about this? Beyond
just being Chinese?

reader, how many times have
I accrued words only to suck
them back through my teeth?

railroads on the West I've yet
to step foot on. museums
I've visited instead, watching Chinese
faces   sealed in black and white.
cooed at by the roman alphabet,
given names and reasons,
statistics in glossy ink.

*Building on the 1875 Page Act, which banned Chinese women from immigrating to the
United States, the Chinese Exclusion Act was the first law implemented to prevent all
members of a specific ethnic or national group from immigrating.*

stuck between

       cages / cages / cages / cages / cages

what gives me   the right
to speak?

             child of the Midwest.   born
to cornfields, suburban rabbits skittering
through summer lawns. rapping my knuckles
on the steering wheel, while outside, dandelion
heads beg to be blown across Newport Road.

every summer, falling into
Pickerel Lake. black hairs sticking
to my neck.   undoing my

swimsuit. stomach, nipple,
body departing land.   holding my breath.

Beyond just being—

Chinese in the twenty-first century. running my fists
through a field of English. playing
S.H.E discs on the red Walkman,
listening to syllables drip like
fat beads of milk into the room.

~

Someday you'll see, she said when she dropped me off at Chinese school every afternoon, and I
walked my slow walk to the vending machines, feeding the black slot green dollars that would
land packs of Funyuns in my lap. Ripping off the plastic. Sucking the MSG off my fingers right
before Mrs. Z entered the room, tapping her fine stick of chalk against the board:

mā má
mǎ mà!

origin points—my body brushing
bursting pushing: *I just don't think*
of you as Chinese, one man
said,   when prompted to answer   the question.

it's not   something I see.   O say.

can you. can you

by the dawn's early light?

dahlias weep their bright red heads, and I take the shears to cut, cut.   try
to imagine it.   Chinese people given small chunks
of land and told, like dogs,   where to stay.

≈

I pledge allegiance. to carbonated water. to rotted
leaves within vases. to the outhouse. *You speak
Chinese? Wo Shuo De Zhong Wen Bu Hao.*

I writhe within a plot of guilt:

You're not from here, are you
at the fish market where I stood off
to the side

sea cucumbers lay
in sheer boxes of ice.

≈

my eyes itch.

I pledge to see.

≈

1882.

*Poster announces passage
of the Chinese Exclusion Act.*

"HIP! HORRAY!
CHINESE EXCLUDED.
Hip! Hurrah! The White Man

is on TOP. Let every DEMOCRAT
and all other GOOD Citizens
turn out and Ratify
this DEMOCRATIC
MEASURE."

≈

Dear [REDACTED,]

I'm interested in exploring your exhibit "   *"*

. . . gathering materials and info from the museum in order to supplement my

[eyes / vision / NEED TO WATCH NEED TO SEE WHAT I AM WRITING MY WAY INTO IS IT OKAY IS IT
OKAY IS IT—

[ASIAN WOMAN, FIVE FEET, PETITE]

[BORN: SEATTLE, WASHINGTON]

[RETAINS ALL TEETH BUT THE WISDOMS]

[VISION: IMPAIRED, -3.50 LEFT, -3.75 RIGHT]

In exchange, I will happily volunteer my:

trust—a horse. a jade piece. will happily dice the spring onions. take me

seriously. take me through museum doors. take these thighs and understand:

how they push me off the ground. how they power and pedal. each morning,

I walk through exhibits and ingest more names. Chester A. Arthur.

Clara Chan Rae Lee. the water lost its carbonation. the water ran its course.

the water has no boundaries, flows from one tongue to the other. see me see

the water. see me bathe and become. *Page Act, cheap Chinese labor, immoral Chinese*

woman, one plaque recites. we can place these words in a textbook and press them

flat. we can rid the vase of its water. dump the flowers down the gutter. American

-born Chinese. looking for answers. *in the name of "research?"* in the name

of belonging? in the name of stitching tight the gulf between   —

                                                 or letting it grow.

                                       ~

scratching my bee sting in front of the open
window   until it bleeds.
pollinator gardens, set up in rows
    along a truck-stained freeway.
yesterday, I ran.   trilliums clung
to my hands.
    these same fingers   once touched
the petals of wild ginger, sepals forming
a purple cup—   now dig into my toe to scratch,
scratch,   surfacing for
        blood.

    I have been writing
about hammers and nails. writing about
hands   which belonged to people
    whose names I can't pronounce.

Angel Island State Park is   *a destination*
                                      a hidden gem
                                      a walk through time
                                      a cattle ranch
                                      a missile base

                                      the rest is history

my toe hardens and swells to the size
of a golf ball.   my memory clams
shut.   once, unwanted men rode boats
          & were asked to wait their cases.
          women pledged their names
          to laws that scratched them out.

all this I know from fact. the shut eye
of   history textbooks, blind
          to what the black font
          does not   want to see.

On Angel Island State Park, we have   *bike rentals (all riders under age 18*
                                               required to wear helmets)

                                               charcoal grills or camp stoves

                                               night travel: prohibited
                                               dogs: prohibited
                                               collecting or destroying anything
                                               in the park (including mushrooms)
                                               : prohibited

I am scratching out the blood
& drawing it across a foot
bumpy thread on skinny terrain
my own my own

(recalling geese
that would glide
easy into the pond
in my Michigan home
my Nainai grinning
declaring she'd catch one
for my sister and me
while we pedaled on bicycles
with purple streamers)

once prohibited by law or nation

                        my body exists here

                        as do ferns
                        as does wind

I have been writing about hands
which carved the words into
a wall   which were not
my parents' hands or those
of their parents'   but the hands
of bodies that came before us:
          fluid, capable.

on the West Coast there are
mountainbells   pinesap
in clumps of bright red
hanging off   the intersections
of tree roots   which these hands
did not   touch   but must
have   touched rock   or water
    must have touched some bone
       in me   my fingers type

21

Angel Island　　　　onto a screen

　　　then click a link on the State Park website
　　　which carries me to a Pinterest board

　　　　　　　　　　　full of Chinese characters
　　　　　　　　　　　carved into the hard rock
　　　　　　　　　　　of barrack walls

　　　　　　　　　　　again, what I can't read:
　　　　　　　　　　　characters I've bent my lips
　　　　　　　　　　　around or scraped against

　　　　　　　　　　　what I can:

　　　　　　　　　　　"shall we have Chinese?
　　　　　　　　　　　NO!　NO!　NO!"

for my body to become some body

it had to understand

when I opened the history textbooks

and read:　　　*Whereas in the opinion of the Government of the United States the*
　　　　　　　　coming of Chinese laborers to this country endangers the good
　　　　　　　　order of

ferns
　　water
　　　　rooftops
　　　　　　　　eggshells pure whites

22

for my mouth to carry English

it needs to understand I am
beholden to other hands
I don't belong to.

still, they touched ground
here. told what was
prohibited (their bodies
teeth houses with tall
pillars that struck
the earth), they
planted characters
in a language
skewered by my stupid
contemporary mouth.
they leaked, scratched the dirt.

they stayed.

LINEAGE OF

NONE ON THE ROOFTOPS

chinese school, year 7 & richard
& grant & gloria & me all cheating
on the midterm with the eraser. she
writes one character on top then passes
it discreetly to me & I pass to the others.
chain. shame. there are no chinese gods
on the rooftops but if there were they
would not be shaped like dragons nor
carrying porcelain bowls of pears. I
believe they would get a good laugh
outta us with our sticky dorito fingers
& our inability to say their names. o
chinese god, are you there, are you
smoking? please hear me out. I am
stupid & young & I like your necklace.
I am asking how come when
emily called me a twinkie I could
only imagine sweet cream smacked
between my thighs, could only
godlessly swallow? how come
when emily called me a twinkie
you didn't say anything about
the blessed stuff like
my nainai chasing a goose for me or
how I learned to pickle cucumbers
in a tin. characters grew gummy wings
in my throat & refused to flit—

                    o chinese god I have a fist.
                    I wanted to be good at this. I
                    wanted not to cheat but

to actually see you standing
there in front of the blackboard
mouthing the proper characters
for *child*, for *forgive*, for *tame*.

EATING AT THE FANCY SHANGHAI RESTAURANT

we go into because we are foreign, and there is everything left.
we've walked the streets: pomegranates, candied apples on
sticks, fish heads cut into blocks and sold, their jelly eyes
lifted toward our bellies. we've walked the indoor markets,
too: touched kites, their knotted strings. toy planes that brandish
their luminous wings. we see skinny insects chirping inside
cages and do not release them with our money, which *could*
buy a whole well, here, a merchant calls out. which could buy
a whole horse here, if we wanted to. we don't want to.
we are tired. we go into the building with its glass sliding
doors and I am thinking of my aunts, how they told me
stories of playing with plastic candy wrappers as young girls.
how èr yí was sent to the countryside for two years
and slept with a light bulb dangling its string above
her head. there were rats, then. there were thieves, too.
one stole èr yí's package of mántou, the white dough kneaded
into hard, sweet circles. another stole her ink pen. the words
are *bare*, and *hunger*, which they do not say. the words are *stripped*
from my tongue. *tell me more / I'm hungry / how much?*

                     I stutter in English, a wingless weight.

at the fancy Shanghai restaurant on the eleventh floor of
the hotel, there is an entire Western Foods section
of the buffet. ham and cheese sandwiches cut into tidy
squares. chocolate fondue melting over a bubbling pot.
my roommate makes way for the grilled steak beneath
the chandelier and I am alone, now, carrying a tray
in my arms which holds nothing—the rich Chinese
folks wearing fur coats and sleeves of silver all around me.

the white folks on vacation, washing their hands. in the next
room, or the next, I can almost hear my aunts laughing, clutching
their bellies, wiping away tears: a chortling of sorts that starts,
at first, like a whinny   then turns into a roar.

"THE SITUATION IS GRATIFYING"

形势喜人
YAN GUIMING, OCTOBER 1974

CHINA: 1970s

i

mao makes thick lines in my red
book. ants make thick lines in
the sand. china makes a thick line
down a stratosphere. my father's name
is a thick belt around my waist. what I
should lose encircles me: chain-link
fence, my sister's face—pruned & pitted
in the dark. last year I carried sweet
potatoes in a barrel & stored them
beneath a bed. last year I sold many
dark hunks of coal. my father came
home & took off his stethoscope.
my father came home & lined
his forehead with sweat. I was
a small line of army ants beneath
the bed. my father was a long line
of men who lost their jobs. I was
fighting for breath when they shut
down the universities. my sheets
stunk with sweet potato. my sheets
stunk. bodies rained sweat. *gratifying*
as in my sister chased me beneath
the persimmon tree but I was
quick, quicker. I descend from
a lineage of flat lines. we compose
a horizon. red pearl as in red sun as in
a father's mouth when he tells us

to shut up, things are *gratifying* while
his eyes cut what is sweet into tiny disks.

ii

there is a myth about monkeys trying
to catch the moon inside a well. their
tails curl around each other as they
lower themselves into the water. they
push wet fists through the moon for
days, & on & on the water ripples.

iii

what I am is monkey. pushing my hand
through the reflection of a moon. a decade.
a persimmon tree with all its leaves shaking
shadows onto yard. what I am is taut
line stitching me to my father, who is
also nation. who is also bone. no spoons
in the household but a rack of skinny
meat. no spoons in the household
but a line of daughters looking
their red books in the eye. *the situation
is gratifying.* the situation slid me across
a sink. my father was my father until
I watched him turn his mouth into
a pearl. soundless when the officer
implied *counterrevolutionary action* & he
said nothing. flattened from my father
into a line of water. they took him away,
made my face river. made
an entire country flood.

POEM FOR CLARA ELIZABETH CHAN LEE

1886–1993

whose ballot was cast into the square box and on it: dark
bullets marking her choice. on the page, the space

was hers: supple and blank. circles to darken.
a dozen ways to show what you stood for.

& what she stood for: a vase of prickly pear
stems. lips smudged to honey & red. a president for

whom she could pledge right hand over chest. she voted
to say the words: *Allegiance to*—the woman she was, bound

in a jacket, smelling the blank smell of soap. *California
Proposition 4, 1911.* the paperwork took one month,

another. her wrists carved out the letters in her name.
boa constrictor of the *L* wrapped around the two

e's. boa constrictor of the law, its tail coiling around
her neck. Clara Lee, first Chinese American woman

to register to vote. the year she died was a year I lived: breathed
puffs of air into my mother's chest. childhood of wet grass

& ink stains. long childhood of spelling my name. English
letters like squiggles, or insects bent at the spine. English

letters crawling over my face. the first time I darkened a circle
on an American ballot, I pressed my hands to my mouth and thought

of her. the long sheath of papers beneath her fists. her fingernails
due for a trim. first woman in the polling booth, choosing. her body

pulling long breaths, electing itself to sign, to sign. to speak.

NAINAI KILLED RATS

in the basement with a broom. we
were kids, feral. gooseberry jam. real
smart lipped. four-square, too. cool
asphalt, shiny sneaker kings. we
watched the rats after she left
for work. tails: gray cords coiled. school
in the basement, slant windows, we
sat near a tipping sun. lurk
of water in a pipe. lurk of blood. late
to the show in sequins, whiskers. we
watched those rats die. a little strike
atop the skull. a little straight
cut. we did not learn *thrash*. we
did not learn *suffer*. to sing
a ribcage like a kettle. to sin
a little, we thought. we
were kids. our world: thin
blots of pink, sun. said the word *gin*!
nothing but a fine rhyme, sliding fast. we
touched the rats, their small jazz
of leaving. it was not until june
that she sealed the pipe shut. we
knew they would die
(and their children, too).
we wouldn't forget, then. but soon.

MY SISTER PLUCKS THE HAIR ABOVE MY UPPER LIP

with tweezers. black hairs sigh. she
splits the roots. my skin real
pink, smarting now but I'm cool

with loss. crouching before mirror we
bargain with what's left—
skin   shine. I'm school

bell, brass bell. alarm, alarm. we
are Chinese & let it lurk,
or pluck. every day a late

pass to the joke, or reminder we
got doors beneath tongue. 段, 段, strike
gold when you say our name. straight

up Mandarin. straight up kitchen sink. we
scrub Chinese out but it grows back   in. sing
alphabets & curly letters to forget but sin

sharpens shame. we erase what little honey we
have 'til our mouths turn thin
in lamplight. our ancestors took gin

& made things with their hands. we
broke apart what they gave us, jazz
on their upper lips in June,

in winter. moustaches & fists. we
refused lineage, left hair   to die
in the sink, whispering *we'll come back come back soon.*

FEAST

each year, we'd set the tables with the butterball turkey.
stuffing & gravy from plastic bins with black lids
we could snap off. supermarket cranberry sauce
congealing in dark red clumps like blood
in the bowl. I loved the stuff. food to silence
my mother, who would withhold, for once,
her telltale *I can make that—*

    on the table, what she couldn't make:
    tufts of mashed potato, bacon crisps,
    green beans the color of saggy office
    couches, brussels sprouts, triangles
    of orange cheese with names
    we couldn't sing—& the soft pats of butter
    glowing like halos atop crackling
    plots of turkey skin.

doorbells rang. my sister and I handed every incomer
a pair of red slippers. I wished badly for a golden retriever
to lick their ankles. I wished badly for hamburgers—whole
towers of them—iceberg lettuce like frilled skirt hems peeking
beneath thick juicy patties. each year, what I got: dinner parties
full of Chinese immigrants. some, my father's students; others,
our neighbors, the Wangs, carrying pans of shrimp doused
in hot oyster sauce. my mother hovered at the stovetop,
anxiously checking the oven for the pumpkin pie to set.
No control, no control . . . she hummed, while my father
scooped up tender flanks of bok choy and laid them gently
into a glass dish, then carried chili-fried peanuts into
the TV room, where gaggles of Chinese wore corduroy or
cotton, mothers shushing their babies who burped or blurted
the alphabet song, the elementary schoolers playing some stray

game of tag, one shattering my mother's statue of a blue
horse, another ramming into the piano bench and releasing
a shrill, goatlike wail. my sister & I ate caramel candies in
a corner and paid our dues: corralling the other seventh graders
into a PG-13 game of Apples to Apples, the heavyweight
music of the kitchen—clangs, splutters, mother's *aiya!* at
the pie, burnt to a sinister crisp—following our
every move. meanwhile, the silver nose of scissors
snipped through a plastic bag of vermicelli noodles.
meanwhile, water sluiced mercilessly from the bathroom
sink. Chinese fathers slapped down cards in
the dining room, shoulders hunched, a collective herd
of bulls rattling their breaths, the jokers making their emergence
at each game's end. *chuī niú!* one father would shout, leaping
out of his seat, bottle of Tsingtao spilling a little arc of sour
beer across the carpet. on the television, a basketball
kissed the net's rim to meet American applause. in
the bathroom, the elementary schoolers, again, filled
the tub with Legos and their cups of fruit punch.

each year, my holidays full of Chinese immigrants
& all their kids: families or young couples or students
who'd later take home my parents' old toaster,
blankets, chess sets my sister & I had grown out of.
I never understood why my mother gave so much away.
bundles of silverware, the microwave from the basement,
which she meticulously cleaned with a dish rag the week
prior. *But don't you wanna keep it?* I'd ask before
the guests came, while she smoothed the creases
of last season's puffy red coat and deposited it into
a paper bag. eavesdropping, my father would laugh.

on the piano, there is a photograph of my parents
decades ago, new immigrants to Seattle, where they'd
collect buckets of clams on the weekends, mistaking
them for oysters. my mother wore

gold hoops in her lobes. my father, a sesame
street t-shirt, slim dark jeans, that laugh.
what they got was given to them: mattress,
carving knife, spool of thread. names
of highways; names of nearby grocery
stores, where they could go
to find pickled mustard leaves
and cabbage.

each year, in a corner of the house, setting
down red cards with the faces of apples,
I'd watch my parents kiss babies on
their cheeks; watch my father haul up
the old blender, repack another machine
into a cardboard box saved for occasions
like these, when the slur of water and time
brought new families to our kitchen,
the turkey puffing in the oven, thick
slices of lotus root frying within circles
of grease. my parents in slippers,
holding the knife against the meat,
carving out what they could.

MARY

she comes back from work and chooses an English name from
an online dictionary and she is not my mother now but *Mary*, patron
saint of blue scrubs   she thrusts her fingers into plastic gloves
and opens patients' mouths   I am spun of floss and alphabet she is
Mary—the M pickles in my gums   patients will trust her
now she says   so should I   I raise my teeth to the light bulb
as letters run down my throat   *chī fàn   nǐ chī le ma   nǐ tīng huà le ma*

    cavities or characters or
    the silver nose of a drill

    my mother a dentist named *Mary* or was it hunger they called her or was it rain?

my bottom teeth, crooked now
from years of eating fried radishes, rice   daughter or *nü er* or fish piercing

its mouth through the hook

I open my jaw and Mary scrubs

I let her call me what she will

PROGRAMMED

it's in the way the light moves, the doctor explains, as wài pó's
eyes follow ours in the summer room, as her legs droop
over a wooden chair, dressed in the cotton pants we'd
placed her in, her chin going soft against our touch.
the times my mother took wài pó's hands
and folded them within hers, whispered, *ma?*
ma? wǒ huí lái le, and wài pó let out
an unmistakable groan: a soft horse, trembling.
we all shouted, then—*she understands!* thinking
about onions and the way she would eat them raw, bucking
into each spicy globe with her teeth, *she understands*,
we pleaded with the doctor, seeing her again in that chair,
her ankles round from years of sitting in front
of the television with its boxed blue noise of kissing
and whales. but the doctor brings us back to her hair: silver.
to her hands: still. we are thinking about our lucy doll,
her hair braided into fine brown knots, plush body caged
in a calico dress of heather and flowers. summers ago,
wài pó took a black brow liner and made two thick, dark lines
above the eyes. *women need eyebrows*, she'd said, returning
lucy to us, the doll's face caught in a perpetual state
of surprise, wài pó migrating to the kitchen away from our
slack girlish jaws to slice a thick head of cabbage, leaves
wedged beneath her bossy palms to a fine pulp . . .
now, in the musty hospital room, wài pó sits strapped
to a chair. the doctor tells us it is the light
she is following with her eyes—not our voices, not
our bodies, *we're programmed like that*, he says, *to follow*
where the light goes, and my mother, now, faces her own
mother, sobbing. wrenches wài pó's hands and presses
them to her face, her nose against her mother's nose,
shouting, *ma? ma? don't you see me? don't you see?*

LEARNING HOW TO CUSS IN
MY MOTHER'S TONGUE

ode to cheese puffs. sundays in chinese school, crushing fine
orange silt, running back to the plastic jar. those words
spreading sticky sheens across our tongues: *huǒ, hóng, hǎo,*

courageous, we clutched erasers and spelling dictionaries
our parents gave us—covers glossed with characters
and the residual stink of dried dates. ode to the big mouth

who sat at the back, yanglun or grant or whatever his crushed
name, rolled from one language to another, wiped of wings, jarring
the teacher when he threw wet balls of toilet paper into the room—

idiot boy! she shrieked, spittled, while the rest of us traced
cheese-grit dust from lunch bags into shapes of stars. a character
our chinese teacher was, telling us about old days spent in the mouth

of a garage, packing crates of oranges for shipments up north. ode to
her childhood crush: those citrus trees, gilded in firm green leaves—she
jarred slices and pickled them with her mother, peppercorn tickling

a tongue she would later use to scold us in our baggy jeans. spelling
out her name on the board in chalk, she tapped a scraggly character
with a cane: *zhāng*, she said, and we dutifully mouthed it back, *z, z,*

zhāng, some of us drawing zebrafish in the margins, crushing ice water
from the bottle. on breaks, at the vending machines, we jostled one
another for a spot at the line, whispering about our teacher's mean tongue,

worrying she'd find us here, scanning the glass case for doritos, funyuns,
spellbound by bags of fat and flour. in class, learning the characters
for *mercy*, or *flame*. on breaks, learning the slow curve of our mouths

around illicit words we thought we'd inherited, ones that crushed us
from the inside out: *huài dàn, bèn dàn, zh—*   *jargon!*
junk! our teacher would trill, *have you no shame?* we tongued

cuss words like creme savers. sundays in chinese school, we cast a spell.
giddy and bad, shameless and foreign, we strutted into characters
and clasped their waists, invited them in to dirty our new mouths.

ANOTHER DECADE, ANOTHER MOUTH

baba tells us the story while we crack salted watermelon
seeds between our teeth. handful after handful, dipping

back into the bowl—roll, scatter, sharp clap as the front
tooth touches one black shell, another. *Who wants*

to make a decision like that? he asks. the crack, the salt,
the air parting as wài pó enters the room as she was

back then, hair streaked with silver, mouth a smudge
of blues and pinks. the needle to save her would cost

a fortune—at the hospital, they stood, made wet
by grief. the lamp yellowed wài pó's wrists. the room, airless.

she did not moan. when she was my mother's mother, wài pó
left milk crackers in enamel bowls. her body stood in cuts

of fabric, buttons snuck over hems. every morning: a rooster
by the sidewalk, crooning its thick head to the trees, and every

night, wài pó by the bed, fanning her daughters with a thin
plastic board, *shuì ya, shuì ya*, their soft mouths going pearly

with spit. imagine: babies' lips, slack buds in sleep. imagine: wài pó
in a house full of girls and salt, dangling the peaches by their stems.

baba eats a watermelon seed, tells it again. wài pó as she was back
then, young and sipping water. or middle-aged, the wool scarf tied

into a sharp little bow around her neck. she was sixteen, and swimming.
she was seventy-one, and soft. spilling across a hospital bed, the years

slurring into puddles by the nape of her neck. clouds and frogs. blue
bracelets and hunger. she taught her daughter to peel potatoes with shards

of glass. in memory, heavy rain gilded a sky. in memory, she stood at
the rink of the pond while big droplets laced the curve of her back.

before she became ill and forgot my mother. before she lost control of her
limbs. before I met her in that immobile brown chair. the drool, the tubes

pulling urine out of her body in thin rivers—before this, she drank from cups
with her hands. baba splits the shells in half, and recounts the doctor's words:

the family had a choice. she could be a whole torso in a wooden chair, leaking
in front of a television. or they could place her, snug beneath the dirt.

baba eats his watermelon seeds and does not skip a beat. *nobody wants
to make a decision like that*, he says. but in the airless room of that airless

summer, the years curdled into each other. the papers crackled on a clean
clipboard, wài pó's name written in fine, straight script. the ground remained

the ground, their feet pushed mercilessly against it. waiting for the clock
to tug the decade forward (the bed pan, the spittle, the times I pressed my nose

to her face and breathed in her stale, milky scent. *wài pó?* I asked, as she
watched me.)   the family grabbed the pen.

DESCENT

she shakes the tambourine because it's what was asked of her.
shiny bells kissing a hard rim. she thought it could be enough.
she was a small garden. she faced the door. slivered persimmons
on plates. her mother singing with a voice that pearled, peel.
something about *cabbage heads and the moon cabbage*
heads and the moon—slow dance. slow dance and remember
how it felt the first time. preparing ginger for the fish, the cut. crust,
a lamprey eel in a silted lake. a father and his gold-sequined
wings. spread, unspread. her hands in love, arranging
cuts of bread on a plate. a film about car exhaust on
the television. a film about a modern family's pain.
wài pó in the other room, immobile brown chair.
human vegetable, zhíwù, plant curling its tips
toward a strip of sun. the soup: canned. a lighter clicking
on, then off, shut again. her mother now: *growing old*
is a difficult thing. the first time she imagined
it: a world without a core. a world without a tambourine,
a hand to instruct. to slice a fillet. to love a man.
to trust a daughter, sliding her into the years,
the curve of a back: faucets, silence. *if wài pó could*
still talk, she would have told you, her mother says.
the underbelly of a leaf, strung
with clear beads of water. wài pó's
drool, dripping in the light.

BABA ENCOUNTERS KNIFE AND FORK

in 1991. from a cloud spun with yolky stars, the monkey
king is watching. he eggs my baba on. it is the year
of science. year of moons set like waxy dollops

of soap. supermarkets sell plastic packs of bacon
by the pound. the hubble telescope pulses through
a sleeve of days and nights. year of baba

on the rise, riding carpeted airplanes across
the sea, young scientist at the lab, invited
to his first American conference.

in Seattle, spirals of cucumber land on baba's plate.
he pulls at wads of white bread, which he rolls
between his fingers into sticky, ant-sized balls. tilt

the scene to find the monkey king sprinkling dust
atop my baba's head, urging him to chew with his
mouth closed, grip the wine glass by the stem.

to prepare for the main course, baba laughs,
the base of his throat turning red like a poppy.
at the table, other American scientists stare

at his hands, *piano man's hands*, mother says,
though baba has never played piano—only
the Chinese fiddle, holding it by the neck

with his eyes closed, letting the syrupy notes
slip into air. see him fumble with the steak.
the monkey king hisses between his fangs

for baba to pay attention, to admire
the flank with its fibers of raw, bloodied pink.
to be a civil creature . . . the monkey king insists,

one must turn to the knife. make incisions.
cut a slab of muscle on a plate. remember
the tea leaf eggs smattered with soy sauce, cracked

so gently with the backs of spoons. recall stems
of bok choy deflating in the saucepan,
the hammock he slept in as a makeshift bed, slung

from the rafters of the house each night. cut the reel.
lose the rice gilded with clots of ginger, lose
the chopsticks humming their two fine shadows

over the lip of the bowl. the monkey king begins
to puppeteer my baba's arms: the fork to stab,
the knife to pry apart, but baba resists, shrugging

him off, letting the silver tools clatter. seizes the meat
between his hands. there's an indent
where he's gripped too hard, the steak's

juice wetting his thumb. but no matter.
from his cloud, the monkey king startles.
his tricks tumble out of his pocket

like crumpled silks falling, falling . . .
his tail twitches with resignation as,
leaning in, my baba widens his jaw,

molars glistening,
and takes
a steady bite—

IN THE MODERN ENCYCLOPEDIA FOR BASKETBALL

men make jump shots and leave blue ink on the pads of my fingers.
there are years of sweet grass. there are years where I dance alone
on a court made of asphalt, and baba tells me to remember I am
great. the fish in the sea splash their teeny tails and cannot touch
me. I'm unstoppable! clogs on my feet, my wingspan stretched
out to the treetops. remembering I descend from a man who once
drove me through the entire car wash: soap suds lingering over
the frame of the car, wiping away crusts of bird shit, dirt, the even
hum of the engine as it propelled us forward, forward. and even then,
I loved to watch a machine grow clean, cleaner. I loved to watch
my baba at the wheel, talking about zebra fish in dishes of cool
water. here I am now, darting between pages—photographs of men
wearing capes that say CHAMPION, only I'm the *champion* now,
rich with sweat. rich as a daughter can be: watching her father's
mouth open into a small pearl as the Chinese opera disc spins. on
the page, the ball falls into the hoop. and he begins, off-key, to sing.

REIN

my baba sits in a midwest
garage with the hood propped

open. blue coolant in a bottle.
small puttering of mice.

one time, yeye died
& I couldn't get him

back. could only watch
the metal twitch, the jumper

cables moan. I wanted
to eat fish. I wanted

a quick fix. one
time yeye died

& my baba tried
to commit a car

to his hands, spun the dial
hard, but it wouldn't

listen. I made baba a cup
of kool-aid. he brought

the sugar to his mouth.
it was the closest we got

to hearing him say it.
I loved, I loved I love a man.

my man. my baba.
fatherless now, &

belching like a horse.
I almost expected him

to nudge yeye with his
snout, turn his body

into warm hay. I love, I
love I love my old

man, huddled over
the car door when

he thinks we're not
watching, his grief

unbuckled & oiling
the leathery backs

of his hands.

I MAKE A NEW SONG FOR MYSELF

i

on I-90, my father and I drive toward my sister.
I count what I see. birds of prey: five. miles to
destination: 611. roadkill: unmeasurable
in pink oblong shapes, set beneath
a sweep of clouds. we unpack the cucumbers
my mother has washed for us and laid into
a plastic box. from the passenger's seat,
I unscrew his water bottle cap, and he
takes a swig, crushing the plastic.
what can I name as *ritual*? a vegetable
peeler, a Midwest cornfield, the maddening
red reel of the sun as it goes down,
down, hushing the interstate country
around us to black. what can I name as ours?

ii

when I came to this country, my father begins,
but I know it is not his first beginning.
what I imagine of his childhood: saltwater fish,
a can of peach syrup, his sisters twisting
their black hair to braids, alive alive. my father's
mother, in her nineties now, tells me across
a phone line to wash my hands. in a gas station
bathroom in Ohio, I hide my mouth behind
a surgical mask, and unclench my fists
obediently beneath the automatic dispenser.
soap falls in a little white puff and I touch
and touch the water, grateful to be touched back.

iii

my father learned how to drive with his American
friend Steve, who owned a blue truck in Seattle.
on an interstate in the late nineties, bound
for an ambiguous horizon line, my father
sat upright, pressed the gas pedal, then flew.

iv

driving to my sister, my father places a baseball
cap in the cupholder. *what's that for?* I ask him,
and he says, *disguise*, catching my eyes in
the mirror and knowing I've seen him, then,
his head full of dyed black hair,
the occasional silver straggler.

we talk of the virus. the death toll. face masks.
whole Chinese American communities
buying guns. in upstate New York, we
roll down our windows for a toll guard,
who asks us where we're going, where
we're from. later, passing by tall
fields of corn, my father comments
that it must be *so sad, to die alone,*
away from your family . . . and trails off, replacing
his thought with a new story: his grandmother,
the toughest of the neighborhood, a woman
not to be reckoned with. *she raised four children,*
he says, *while widowed at age 27, worked in the textile*
factories, made a name for herself.   all this: I didn't know.

v

what   *comes from China*:   my aunt
laughing, joy whistling through the gap
in her teeth.   rain showers. fruit markets.
Nainai in a glittering sweater. my cousins
feeding change to a subway station.

my father's childhood,
pressed between the Yellow Sea
and bowls of ice flavored
with lychee and milk. paper,
and, centuries later,   electric
guitars. sunflower seeds tossed from
the twentieth stories of skyscrapers
for citywide birds.

vi
in Pennsylvania, we stop at a grocery store
full of white people pushing carts down aisles
of frozen casserole, drumsticks, peas, & I
fidget with my mask, feeling outcast
and embarrassed.   *what?*
my father says, then sticks out his hands, bends
an elbow, a leg, beginning to makeshift dance,
lift your head, he says, and saunters
down the aisle in a face mask, a tiny bottle
of sanitizer strung around his wrist, waiting
for me to catch up.   back
in the car, bladders emptied and face
masks off, we start to drive. *what
are you ashamed of?* he asks. *you can choose
to be small, or you can choose to be brave.*
so I make a new song for myself
and all my selves, lined up next
to my Chinese father beneath one gray
sky, rolling past the roofs of food
banks, American crows, weeds
prancing—soft, golden arrows
cast in wind.

WÀI GŌNG IS DANCING

in a wool cap. in the bathtub. on market streets & in
the fat doorway of his first home, where jars overflow
with melon candies & a bicycle with a broken bell sags
against the window. he's dancing in the soccer field,
the sweet potato cellar, the narrow hallway of the nation's
seventy-fifth public school. outside: a flagpole, a lone sea-
gull. the bell rings & boys billow past. my wài gōng
toe-taps, does a grapevine jig, caws for their
attention but the boys see past him, his swollen
body, his parched mouth. so he's dancing into
our homes now, watching one of us braid abby's
hair to dark twists & turns. dà yí lights the stovetop,
mutters a few words as the match sparks, then soots
to black in her palm. & there's wài gōng again,
levitating against the pot of green peppers & tapping
his heels together, making that strange clanging sound,
vying for us to see. the fish in the tank gurgle. the milk:
sucked through a straw. *when's the baby due?* the distant
cousin asks my cousin, and her mouth opens into a slow
moon, letting the breath fall out. leaving the house, then,
wài gōng sways into the yellow sea, tucking his arms behind
his back, vein-striped legs punching the brine. he's chortling.
the vendors hawk cheap souvenirs: fake pearls coiled
into rings, dried squid packaged into plastic sacks.
the ocean dips and folds him up, giddy, delicious,
& wài gōng laughs & laughs & laughs & laughs
a laugh of fake teeth, soaked each night, for decades,
in clear sanitizing solution. last night, he died. we all
leaked a little light, watching him go, his granddaughters
& daughters, only a few of us by his side, the rest
scattered across the water, nestled into new tucks of land . . .
he lifts himself up. ocean, peach, sunlight approaching

grave, water, grandfather dancing, eating oranges
we'll eventually leave for him at his tomb, joss sticks
we'll roast 'til the red paper money smokes his way rich.
wrapped in a flag, he dances. somewhere out there, he
presses the boom box, silver buttons primed to play.
pray. *so much to feast on, in a life*. the intimacy
of breath, the rippling kindness of white dough,
the forward slope of the living. past,
past it all, wài gōng slow dances.
the waves fill with salt, then spray.

LOVE POTION

at the Asian Dinner Party, every Chinese auntie
pinches my cheeks & tells me I've lost weight.

lotus root in bone-white plates. dumpling wrappers
pressed with flour, steamed slick and covering shy

spheres of chive, mushroom, pork, beef. I was raised
here. in between kitchens of my mother's friends'

homes, listening to my aunties bestow love potions
on spoons. bites of dried date or sticky rice bricked

with sweet red bean: benedictions that someday, I'd
marry a tall doctor in a clean coat, an engineer making

big bucks in a Bay Area lab. I was smaller, then,
and wanted to be a *writer*, carrying around a notebook

to every dinner and documenting what I ate. *beef broth,
celery buns, tiny wafers tasting of seaweed, and salt.* what I'd give

to hoist my plate full again. to kiss each auntie on her
wizened cheek. knowing what I know now: my body

made possible by a daughter of a daughter of a daughter,
my mothers before me, across oceans, recalling papery

ration cards, the kindness of persimmon trees,
their mothers at textile factories bending & unbending

their wrists. *I just want you to live a good life,*
my aunties used to say, speaking with such pursed

lips, hauling out dough beneath their hands for
yellow cakes later rolled with cream and berries,

imitations of white people's confectionaries
at the chain grocery store on another aimless

suburban road. what I'd give to write them, now.
sweet love potions for my aunties. scoot those imagined

men out of those rooms. line the shelves full of eggs, or
brown sugar. milk powder, bread. I don't care

about your paintings of tiger mothers. you can say
what you will; these women fed me with their hands.

I was smaller, then, and did not know hunger.
in July backyards, my aunties filled picnic tables

with barbeque ribs, Chinese sausages in neat, pink
rows. they cast love potions for me while

slicing seedless watermelons to wet, red songs.
in their mouths fit prayers or the improbable

stuff of roses, dreams. but say what
you want. my aunties. they made a world

for me in their kitchens.
they taught me how to live.

PORTRAIT WITH BOK CHOY IN PAN

my sister plucks leaves, chops them atop the cutting board.
green blurs beneath the water. when we were small,
we'd clasp our bowls with two hands, calling for
yóu cài! yóu cài! eyeing those shimmery fine stalks
slanted on top of rice. I was raised to be a sister.
see the oil swim, the oyster sauce spreading
its sheen above the lip. she casts the pepper
like a spell: shake, unspool. first the vegetable oil,
then the garlic cloves, the generous smatter of salt.
what we love, we run like oil over skin: stovetop air,
light dressing our wrists, slender leafy things arcing
toward the roof & made all tender once oil strikes
the pan. she guides the spatula, coaxing them to cook,
thinking *green and steady, river of oil,* eat, eat, eat.

INHERIT WHAT YOU CAN

DO YOU HAVE A GRAMMATICALLY CORRECT RESPONSE TO THE QUESTION?

—and remember the time I stood at the intersection
carrying my black suit of hair and the woman stopped in
her shiny car, rolled down her window to scream something
vulgar something clanking inside her mouth a word a system
of grammar flipped to   fury red ripe railing at me?

   for what? my body?   my attention?

Anger is often in response to a boundary crossed . . .

what was that boundary? where were my legs? why did
I stand there, without a word, holding the straw in my ice-
cubed drink as the liquid turned warm & illegible between
    these jaws? slosh,

  slosh,

  the woman stopped in her shiny car.
  the woman stopped to scream   "_____!"

                "_____! You _____!"

            in her shiny car

            at me.

Who is the subject of this sentence? Who is the object? What is the verb?

Standard English Grammar dictates . . . the proper tense.
                  do I care about the proper?

she spat at me. she said a bad word. a string of words demarcating

my body *(hit by grammar, hit by a field of letters, hid behind a lump*
in my throat while my body remained my body, my lungs pulled up
the hot July air, my hair remained parted to the side as I clasped
the straw as I watched   the tips of my feet) a body to be screamed
at by a stranger.   July, North American. a street.

Which tense would you like to use to describe the incident above?

(the past)   the future.

I will eat leaves and pour vinaigrette
slow & skinny. I will feed the low opal of my mouth. in times of
distress, I will turn on the stove. garlic will be fried in a river
of yellow oil. I will eat my letters, crunchy and fat. angry
and swollen, soft and slathered in old-fashioned oats, I will
try to pull up the words:

 Hit me she did. Hurt me I am.
 Language she did.

 The word _____ I am.

                              am not.

on a North American street, on a hot
July day, a woman stopped her car
where I waited at an intersection to
tell me I was a _____.

on a North American street, on a hot
July day, a woman stopped her car
where I waited at an intersection
to scream the word _____!

later, I wilted leaves in a hot pan.
later, I fed the story back
to my mouth. later, the syntax
was rewound in a reel, set aside,
and I composed a new body
of roman letters out of
my body—I pulled up words
from their waggling roots
and raised them to touch
the edges of a face, a page,
to cure and hold and praise
and wriggle and snap and sister
and (alive!) amen
and (alive!) amen

then defy and defy and   talk back.

THE THEMATICS OF BLOOD

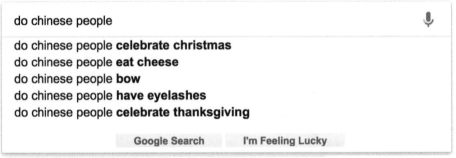

do chinese people

> do chinese people **celebrate christmas**
> do chinese people **eat cheese**
> do chinese people **bow**
> do chinese people **have eyelashes**
> do chinese people **celebrate thanksgiving**

Google Search   I'm Feeling Lucky

Report inappropriate predictions

sit proper. raise a glass. call somebody *baobao*, then wipe their soft
baby cheek. drink milk tea at dusk. or never at all. tapioca bubbles
slick black & glistening, like fish eggs stuck between cubes of ice.
he recounts the time a Chinese student bowed, with his hands to
his heart: *like this,*   like this   :

so crack the heart, figgy, over a bowl. whole seeds in a mouth
to unswallow, spit back up. surface for air. brush the cake with
egg yolks, or bash the cake in with a fist. no oranges twined
with green leaves. here, no gentle touch. an egg turns solid
under heat. a person—liquid, private. full of hungry eyes.

once, in Xi'an: a backpack filled with donuts, sugar flecked gold.
rinds of melons, glazed ducks, flies plump and humming near
a silver fishing line. once, in Qingdao: the women's sharp caws
of *ai-ya!* as the low tide came in, pouring salt water across their
plastic sandals. *this is an opportune moment*, he said. *a photo, a photo—*

do not take his photo. let the hot water in the pan cool, cease
to ripple. then take out the trash. a search engine pulls up
a body, quivering and mean. send it gliding across a plain.
the truth is sweaty—say it, still: *yeye was a basketball player.*
nainai grew radishes, and sliced them into spicy discs. on the fifth floor

of a brick building—inherit what you can. stick the tongue,
a selfish muscle, out to meet the world. there, can you taste
it? salt, a heated coin, an eyelash falling, falling . . .

do Chinese   people   celebrate

        eat   —have?

"CAN YOU SPEAK ENGLISH YES OR NO"

always hurled out an open car window. from a bus stop. a door
opening to a friend's home. her parents set the table. bone
china and a polished casserole dish. always, the picture book splayed
open, revealing an illustrated apple, black seeds, gnawed over
by caterpillars. always my face, which is not enough.
my tongue, which curls and curls and remains tethered.
letters coiled like grape vines around the tip. roman
alphabet digging at the space between my gums. consonants
dropped like bricks, I chew their weight. always some man
telling me what I am, what we already know. *say it right / say
it / say—can you read / can you speak / English / English / yes,*
no. in this story, always, I am jumping over parts, skipping
them. can you see me. can you see. I entered the car and turned
off the engine. I looked into his face. I opened my mouth and let
it all roll out: a spell, an incantation, *hiss / miss / fist /* a caterpillar
slung off a silken web. today I am what I always am. girl
who brays! or prays!   when I swallow, watch
where the spit goes. down a throat, a chest, a rib.
witness it. my sly, unbreakable bone.

PIN1YIN1.COM

in the family chat, my mother texts another
neat block of Mandarin.   I offer her words
to the internet. contemporary chapel. lord   forgive me

   for cheating

   again: the translation box greedy
   for my copy, paste.   like an obedient
             owner being
             walked on a leash,
             I feed it text.

梯子 reading *tī zi*   meaning *ladder.*

带回来 reading *dài huí lái*   meaning *bring it back.*

哎呀 reading *āi yā!*   meaning reader, I don't want to be
                  your machine.   see

   my mouth forging the round in me (a fish)   to an

                                    O, O.

                             I pulse. remember

English, *-glishhhh*, *-lishhh*, *-shhh*, ESL class for half a year
as a kid. the curtains parting, then obscuring. tongue
I was raised in—cordoned, wiped away.

now, words I have no Chinese equivalents for:
the papery powder atop a eucalyptus leaf.   the pores

69

like pepper dots atop a distant relative's nose.
sex.   anthropology.   this drying bed of grass:

                                resident on my tongue.

relegated to the roman alphabet, I only
know   phonetics:

            mā má
            mǎ mà!

years ago, at the chicken restaurant in Beijing, I squinted
at the menu.   *I want this one*, I said, pointing, and the waitress
gave me a steady stare before bringing over an ambiguous plate.

SITTING ON A U.S. BENCH, A MOSQUITO TAKES MY BLOOD

& I smack only to reveal red juice, sucked. blood
on the back of my palm. I'm vine-thick with stars. my blood
pulses when I sip water, break an insect into my fist. blood
lines knotting me to a country full of cement. blood
orange on my lip—come apart in wedges, liquid on a tongue. blood!
or run. or inflate this country with your *yearning to breathe*   . bloody
my mouth with questions, like *how does history sit down despite the blood
in her lap* or *can watchdogs tell when you are afraid?* I'm afraid. my blood
is not neutral. my blood swims away. pollinates, gets kissed. blood
marking my mother's passport blue with wings. *Naturalized Blood*
for all this nation deems "natural"—a white house, a fence, blood
darkened on a cutting board, a lit-up street. fat hum of sirens. bloody
nation that sleeps. & sleeps. chains to its leash. how to say *blood*.
how to say *amen*. I won't mean it. I'll bleed when I'm bit, I'll pledge blood
but not today, not to this country with its history making blood
sport of our oceans & wrists. look, a flower. look, a blood
moon. a dog's ribs, gaunt. gleaming beneath light. my blood
in a file, gathering up dust. my country's name on my lips.

guilty with blood.

I-94

& I remember the bus driver who once used each
broken windshield wiper as a drumstick, clattering
on the window, banging out a drum, drum, *who
let the dogs out!* he cawed, and us schoolkids
in the back: feral, baby teeth fallen & craters
between our gums, *who! who, who who who*
we pushed back, & the window grimy with
dust & the strange green branches of maple
& yeah, Lawrence ramming his knee
into my seat, the hard knob
hitting my lower back.   how I
felt it, even then.   what   set me apart
from those other dogs.   I was girl. mouth
unlike those other mouths that moaned or barked.
my throat for speech. pristine beneath a cotton collar.
Lawrence kneeing the back of my seat
until I mumbled the words.   he wanted
to hear me   say it. sitting on the edge
like that. dropping syllables like I
meant them,   *who let*
the dogs   out?   my eyes straight   ahead.

his breath   on   the back of my neck.

our bus full of dogs. or fangs. wheels round

& round. boys became men who forced

it out of me then shrugged:

   who, who,   who   who?

ALL THE MOUTHS OF MEN I'VE LOVED

who've lined their lips with grease at the bbq restaurant, letting fatty
runes of pork shine their cheeks. what they've let slip out: deep

belches, proclamations of care they won't keep, puffs of breath on my neck
as tart and quick as piano keys. cuss words aimed around my head.

lies, smooth and quick, followed by the forked tongues of serpents.
Sweet Babys and sleek sentences gilded with *no*. watch what

these mouths ingest: chicken wings cut inelegantly with the edges
of forks, then ground against molars. buzz words harvested

straight from theory books, thrown around like expectant bones:
patriarchy, gender equality, they chant. *Audre Lorde, bell hooks*.

they drop women's names like coins into a well—plunk, plunk, plunk.
watch these mouths hunt: perform the words, binding them in

spiders' silk. letting their webs sway softly in the breeze. *Angela
Davis. Equal Pay*. in the mouths of men I've loved, letters snag

on rays of light, then glint. vowels stretch their calves. the spiders'
webs remain sticky. and slowly, the mouths inch toward their prey.

in a long year, cloistered in a white room, I sit
with all my mothers perched atop my tongue.

āi yā! my mothers swing their legs, keeping watch like tower guards.
all the mouths of men I've loved begin to file in. *justice!* one man cries,

stretching his thin lips through a megaphone. *gender equality*, another
declares, as a low burp begins to form in his throat. *here we go*, my mothers

snicker, jostle one another in line. one man's mouth yawns wide open, revealing
a soft pink tunnel. focused, my mothers begin to shoot their pucks of ice.

ha! they shout, as the puck sails into a man's throat, preventing the word
from falling out. *zing!* my mothers holler, while another puck cracks

the brittle syntax in half. targeting the meat of male speech,
my mothers flex their biceps, keep score, then dance beneath the roof

of my mouth. all night long, I feel them partying in there. waving their sticks
above their heads. singing glory hymns, while pucks slide, slam, keep—

ARETHA FRANKLIN SINGS "AMAZING GRACE" IN A SEQUINED WHITE TOP

& suddenly, I forget every man who's ever left me on
the side of a bed, curling into myself. forget the men
with their clean fingernails who've told me I'm worth
a speck of dirt or worse, erased me into stale air;
the institutions full of men who've ripped
me off. Aretha sings and beads of sweat
trace her jaw and fall relentlessly into the earth. *amazing*
grace, how sweet the sound of women who've worked
to scrub their names back into themselves. women who've
tunneled the dark sides of their mouths, who've been
placed by men near microphones and instructed to
open, who've opened at their own accord and called
themselves better. I'm better. Aretha makes me believe
in my dirt again. all thousand specks of me, singing
out of an opal mouth. I'm dirty, I'm dirty, I'm precious
and I'm lucky. *I once was blind but now am found*
by a woman with a mouth. a woman with a vocal
chord to command, command. Aretha Franklin
sings "Amazing Grace" in a sequined white top
& suddenly, I remember the muscle in me,
my stovetop whistle. this morning I cracked
an egg over a sizzling plot of butter to feed
my body & called myself Woman, Woman,
reveling in my dirt. impressing even the soil,
who carries radishes and beet sprouts. impressing
even the windows, now open and spangling with light.

POSSIBLE

now my dress smells like rain & all day long: I've been
eager to get back to my book. a novel about a young
couple making pasta & falling into one another's
skin. an Irish novel, with names of cities that clunk
around in my mouth—cities I'd never heard of
but now ride my skull like pleasant, individually
wrapped candies, words with strange cactus-like
shapes, words I star: *Sligo*. *Carricklea*. I turn
the page. my mind goes: stick, stick, stick,
my brain goes hungry for more. today I run
through the rain in my wooden clogs & pleasure
at the sound: thump, thump, thump, the entire
green world of a street flashing down an open
sewer drain. *so alive!* I think, then
remember what else makes me possible: public
libraries. cartilage. a good hardcover. a prayer
I overhear my cab driver mumble while
passing by a full school bus. goose bumps I get
from reading my old journal, one sentence,
another: *my heart is a skull zone* (did I really
write that?)—& oh, I am possible again. I am
a fragrant, silly self. today, I thank
the worms who eat the dirt who
break down the soil who make
the lilacs possible and young, forever
purpling, forever cradled in my palms as I cross
Blakemore Avenue and it rains, rains, rains, and I
think about eating up the alphabet, which has
made a city into a word into a sound: *Sligo*,
which slides, slinky-like, into my brain,
the dear alphabet which has made me
into a woman who will cross the street

and love the lilacs and treasure the strange
turn of the day, the strange turn of
a word, a sentence, a curve and a stroke
of black ink that—thank you—brought me here.

ON MACKINAC ISLAND, I CAST A SPELL

summer in Michigan with my hair up and my neck
released to the wind, breathless flap & gild of fish
skin sitting in ice chips at the market. a dog remains
chained to a skinny pole. a woman spikes a ball
fast over the net. o, riverbed. o, sash tied around
my neck. o, lips I part as I walk past a new body
of water and love what I love and stir it all into
a cauldron: eggplant, plastic fork, black & wet
eye wedded to the water. I fashion a kite
out of old skirt hems. I push two silver
buttons through my earlobes. I admire
the rows of produce: yams, beets, onions,
roses plump with green veins. a day is juicy
with clouds. a body, juicy when kissed.
summer in Michigan with air parting delicious
for my knees as I roll down the hill on
a blue bike, past the horses pattering clip-clop
along a dirty street, past the fudge shop thick
with blocks of sugar, on my bike I roll & I roll
& I fall, tumble near the lake, where a garden
snake hunkers on the shore & my breath goes
up, then down . . . these lungs: winged instruments
I take into my body, then let fly.

AT THE PORTLAND ROSE GARDENS,
I'M PUT IN MY PLACE

menstrual blood slides down my thighs in little jellylike clots

the same way it's slid out of me for years. bursts of blood

up mountains. down hills. in the cable car of a Chinese city,

my distant cousin spoke. *a woman's energy is potent*, she said.

at high elevation, I bled while the ground swayed, trees

mudded with foxes and the high cries of laughingthrush.

that summer, he laid me down on a towel. we thrashed

against each other on a hardwood floor, the blood

molten, rushed, alive alive. after, our hands streaked

with red. the room smoldered, and he cracked

a window for the fingernail moon.

days later, in an international airport, I gripped

the white stick and let my urine tell me

what it did. those spare minutes before peeing,

something ugly unseeding my chest. *won't*

want can't want blood, blood, blood come back.

a year older, I am still potent. on a morning

opened up by sky as bare as I've ever

seen it. on this side of the country, far

away from him, there are no clouds.

there are only my dark strings

of red dangling, like tapestry

thread, into the toilet's wet bowl.

to bleed. to rinse. to watch my red labor

pulse, invent. at the Portland Rose Gardens, I tussle

the pink heads of a new species. *Damask, Redleaf, Prairie,*

Musk, pollen clumped in swollen yellow globes. I am

here, and living, which means I can forgive

that summer now. and everything I can't yet say.

I am here, and living, which means this morning

I take my blood for a walk through the gardens—where

crops of creamy roses lift themselves to my hands, and my red

makes what it does, sliding out of me and into

the bushes, craning its elongating thread.

ATTENDING COMPLINE SERVICE AS A NONBELIEVER

wearing ripped jeans & clogs while onward,
women part their lips and let loose the song. lord
have mercy. it has been a long year. and the rosé
has tripped from a glass cup, slosh-sloshed down
my waiting throat. prayer as night falls.
for memory to unreel, peel back. for grief
to release its thick hold. in a room full
of candles, I forget myself.   amen, the glossy
notes keep ringing. once, I was younger. baba
and I walked through the Galleria dell'Accademia.
David stood, a body suspended in pristine
white. glory in the calves, in the straight
spine. what he didn't own
ran through my body: the low mud
of speech. years later, speaking to men
I loved, I said what I didn't mean.
let words drip out of me like fat
beads of milk.   I said I would
forget, but here, memory muzzles
desire, covers me in its pelt.
in the dark pews
of a church I don't belong to, I come
apart.   made alien tonight
by a river of sound, unwinding
itself through one ear, sticky before
exiting   the
other.   lord, look at what
I've made.   in a year designed
by loss, still, I watch white moths
flicker toward the light. I wrench
open my mouth   to say it:
     in me lives

an entire spool of thread:　　　I am
a daughter of a daughter of a daughter
of a daughter　　　and yes, they
survived so I could sit on a bench
in another country　　　watching
women pry open their lips to leak it
out:　　*as it was in the beginning*
　　　　as it always is
　　　　I begin with a woman
　　　　inside of me
　　　　turning on the lamp
　　　　reciting the words.
　　　　　amen, amen.

DEAR TINDER SCREEN

here I go curating myself on the internet again.
clouds and balloons. stupid photos stacked
mercilessly next to one another, black hair shiny
& teeth tucked neatly into my gums. I want to be
respected. I want to be cherished. please respond
to my texts about the moon. please savor each strand
of my greasy, thinning hair. someday I will grow old
and silver like the rounded edge of a spoon. someday
I will flip a pillow, say TODAY IS GOOD then roll
over in my bed like an overcooked beet. I am
tender if I want to be. I am hopeful when I have
a joke to tell. say the word *jellyfish* watch it slow
dance slow dance. my tongue goes airy. drizzle, flick.
on a good morning I demand oatmeal for breakfast.
I like it best with fat raisins and vitamin D milk.
let's toast pumpkin seeds. let's hold hands. but
know this: I will not pretend to like your dog. I am not
attracted to your hands snagging a fish, its mouth begging
the air for another breath, pink-lit & pulsing O, *oh*.
are you hungry? I'll bake you cookies. three sticks
of butter, store brand. I won't give myself away
and glide, glide. a girl is not a kite. a girl is not
a flyaway hair, a funny tickle at the back of your throat.
I hydrate myself in the mornings,
the GOOD mornings when my phone screen
is black yet my body is full & glinting with sugar, with
pixels of light. I curve myself toward a window
humming some song about herds or basketball
hoops while the wind ruffles me up, turns my hair
into a flag, swinging me on, on,
coopless in my glory, boundless in my solo
shiny   widening self.

VISION WHILE RUNNING ON THE VANDERBILT INDOOR TRACK

three minutes in, & those I've dared to call *god*
in my mind push me on: teresa teng, clara lee,
my nainai, clad in blue silk slippers,
shouting *go! go!* while my will
sags into the folds of a wet tank top.

brown track. white shoelace. blue, smooth love I had
for the river I flew past on a train last spring—
returning to a square room with somebody who
wrapped gifts for me & left them in a pile
on the wooden table, books about olive
trees shying beneath shimmering
sleeves of paper, but—*shhhh!*

nainai sits on the bridge of my nose, telling me
to shut up. *wallowing in heartbreak won't serve
you a mile*, she snaps, and I'm sluggish, heavy,
panting a thousand hurried breaths, watching
the basketballs sail in lean arcs below the track,
the clock flashing red pixels, the ceaseless dribble.

when I think   *I can't survive*
the next minute, the next hour, February with all
my lonely and beads of sweat . . . women slip
into their clouds and chop off their hair, let it
hail over me—black stuff the scent of licorice
& steam. I'm running carrying these women
in my shoes, on my back. they're hollering
my name, cracking into me like oyster shells
with wild tongues, clacking sets of teeth.

I can't   *go on*, I try to tell them, but
they're playing pool in my mouth, saliva
beads & I swallow, tiny women in
my stomach telling me they're
the boss of me now, go *run*   *run* the way
they did all those years ago   nainai
learning how to read by salvaging newsprint
from the factory's lean bins, deciphering
the curly characters, *she her hers*   mouthing
the words for *chain*
change   running
her way to night class after canning
each aluminum tub of peaches

clara elizabeth chan lee running
to the polling booth   her name laid
fresh on a sheath of paper
run   gripping the ballot
tight in her fists   darkening
bubbles   tracing each letter's
swoop & curl   *I choose*
I choose I choose—

teresa teng running to a microphone, her
tongue flitting between Mandarin, Hokkien,
Cantonese, English, high notes strung
like lines of syrup across a room:
    nǐ wèn wǒ ài nǐ yǒu duō shēn?
run! into the moon or into the song
girls would swing into, decades later,
eating bagels with cream cheese at the car
wash, teresa's voice shrill & hopeful,
discography blasted on loop

run, the women in me chant
enclosing me in earthbound duty

'til I'm whirring   midflight
leaving behind one step   one
thousand   *run*
I'm loved,   I love
run 'til   I can't feel
the ache in me anymore, and I'm not
lonely, I'm not lonely, I'm stuffed
to the seams with old laughter, throngs
of it, a line of women in my chest, urging
me to let it fly, blessing me to move
move   move!

SAY A LITTLE PRAYER

a thousand prayers about the red: warm river I catch
between my thighs and clamp to stay. look at me,

glinting: the day writing itself all over my ankles.
this morning, the slow loop of my arms in rain, rain,

rain. shaking my wingspan to release those quick
slick laps. today I stand in a bathtub in Tennessee

with my mouth: its damp cave.
a woman, bleeding. a woman making drops

of moisture across a floor. wetted by a cloud,
& hungry after. I peel off my shirt, then reach

for the words, lather the spaces between & beneath.
conjure back the language for who I am, what

I know, my lips rounding into diphthongs,
my tongue taming itself around a word's slick bead.

what can a woman's tongue grow?
mammoth garden of consonants

& slurred vowels. loose fricatives & a sky
edging its way past the roof of her mouth.

the tongue knows: it is daughter
of a mother of a mother of a mother.

daughter of their swooning rivers, protection
spells, whisks & metal spoons.

a woman's tongue: boat of rage. throne of tenderness.
pricked, plucked, depositing firm commands & refusals

down a drain. standing, bare backed, with every
thing in my mouth: knead & laugh, water

& grow, all of the women in me
singing   *go*. reaching

for the small crest of almond-scented soap.
I lather my own ridges. the water flashes

with pink. bare & new, wet & hungry,
I speak, & it is delicious.

ACKNOWLEDGMENTS

Many thanks to the editors and readers of the following publications, in which versions of these poems first appeared:

Academy of American Poets: "Do You Have a Grammatically Correct Response to the Question?"

Alaska Quarterly Review: "I-94," "Attending Compline Service as a Nonbeliever"

Black Warrior Review: "Mary"

Cosmonauts Avenue: "Dear Tinder Screen"

Frontier Poetry: "Portrait with Bok Choy in Pan," "On Mackinac Island, I Cast a Spell"

Gulf Coast: "Alien Miss Reads Section 14"

Hayden's Ferry Review: "At the Portland Rose Gardens, I'm Put in My Place"

HEArt Online: "My Sister Plucks the Hair above My Upper Lip"

Michigan Quarterly Review: "Alien Miss at the Immigration Station"

Narrative Magazine: "Eating at the Fancy Shanghai Restaurant," "Another Decade, Another Mouth," "Rein"

Peach Magazine: "In the Modern Encyclopedia for Basketball," "'Can You Speak English Yes or No'"

Pleiades: "Programmed"

The Rumpus: "Nainai Killed Rats"

Shallow Ends: "The Thematics of Blood"

Southeast Review: "Wài Gōng Is Dancing"

They Rise Like a Wave: An Anthology of Asian American Women Poets (Blue Oak Press): "Poem for Clara Elizabeth Chan Lee"

Tupelo Quarterly: "Alien Miss"

Winter Tangerine: "'The Situation Is Gratifying,'" "Learning How to Cuss in My Mother's Tongue"

"Nainai Killed Rats" won the Bain-Swiggett Poetry Prize at the University of Michigan; the "Alien Miss" series won the Hopwood Theodore Roethke Prize at the University of Michigan; "Do You Have a Grammatically Correct Response to the Question?" won the 2019 Academy of American Poets Prize at Vanderbilt University; and "Rein" won First Place in *Narrative Magazine*'s 30 Below Contest in 2017.

~

Thank you deeply to many spaces and people, who have helped me envision these poems with power and with clarity. I am a constant student of your love.

Knowing that the act of gratitude is forever live and evolving, I bow and say thank you to those who are yet unnamed in this manuscript—and acknowledge those on the path still ahead of me. While this book is reflective of my interior landscape in the limited years of its making, I am humbled to have learned from, listened to, and loved so many people and places in the years before its creation, and in the years to come. I have reckoned with what it means to create a "book" wherein these stories may be read as "final." To me, the stories in *Alien Miss* are not final, and I am grateful that my learning in these poems—as well as the loves that inform them—continue on.

To my teachers & mentors, who have been generous beyond measure in sharing conversation, counsel, and education: Meg Sweeney, Anne Curzan, Nate Marshall, Tung-Hui Hui, Jeremy Chamberlin, John Whittier-Ferguson, Aisha Sabatini Sloan, Ben Tran, & Anne Gere. Thank you. Special thanks to the Neutral Zone, and to my first poetry teacher, Jeff Kass, for always (courageously, profoundly) passing the mic to the young people.

Thank you to the Vanderbilt MFA Program for providing the resources, space, and time to grow my intellectual gardens, and to write this book. Thanks to Mark Jarman, Kate Daniels, and Rick Hilles for your teaching. A special and dear shout-out to my MFA community of readers and writers who keep my faith in poetry alive, and in doing so, fueled my heart in Nashville—with particular thanks to Elena Britos, John Shakespear, Maddy Parsley, Joanna Currey, and Joshua Moore.

Gratitude to the kind editorial community at the University of Wisconsin Press—including Ron Wallace, Sean Bishop, Dennis Lloyd, Jennifer Conn, and Sheila McMahon—who helped this book sprout its wings. My heartfelt thank you to Mai Ta for your artistry and for inviting me into your creative lineage. What a joy to create alongside you.

Thank you, Michigan writing communities, the Sundress Academy for the Arts, Tin House, DreamYard, Winter Tangerine, Juniper Writing Institute, the University of Michigan Joint Program in English & Education, the Hopwood Program, and Signal Fire Arts for supporting this work.

Thank you to my students—past, present, future. I am honored to grow together.

I am lucky to live a life filled with rich, meaningful friendships. Thank you to the many friends I hold in my heart. I have learned so much about tenderness, abundance, and the action of courageous love from each one of you. A bouquet of gratitude.

I am very thankful for the following writers, readers, and artists who provided feedback on various drafts of this manuscript and many of whom wrote/created work alongside me. You inhabit these pages: Sophie Stid, Jasmine An, Maria Isabelle Carlos, Marlin Jenkins, Molly Raynor, Courtney Brown, Grace Ludmer, Yaoyao Liu, & Bea Troxel.

My gratitude to Yusef, for holding me with patience and deep kindness.

∿

The writer EJ Koh wrote: "'You know my grandmothers,' I said, and pointed at my nose, a habit I had picked up when I lived in Japan. 'I'm an accumulation of their lives. Whatever I say or do now can give relief to the past—and to them. I don't believe they're gone.'"

This book is one big love poem to my family: To my grandparents and my cousins, to my uncles and my aunts, to my grandmothers' mothers, to their mothers before them. You've made your thousand ways into my thoughts and have consequently paved gold.

To my parents, who are constant sources of support, wisdom, courage, generosity, and incredible strength: Your love and your sacrifice render me powerful and living. I am proud to be yours.

And to Karen: The poet Angel Nafis writes, "put my name next to her name / and said look at this girl your / whole life and know some kind / of peace." Which is how I feel every day, knowing you. I thank the world that gave me my sister.

NOTES

In the "Alien Miss" sequence, I explore the intergenerational histories of Chinese American immigrants in the United States, as affected by the "official record" of legal rhetoric and historical "fact." Alien Miss is a part-fictionalized, part-autobiographical figure composed of my own reading, research, and personal experience. Through this sequence, I ask: *Who is permitted to write (and hold) history?* Through "Alien Miss," I hope to honor Chinese American men and women who were named and unnamed in historical records, as much as I hope to expand my own understanding(s) of inheritance, accountability, survival, and lineage—a lineage that includes injustice and violence, as much as it encompasses joy. All errors and opinions in this sequence, as well as throughout the book, are my own.

"Alien Miss" is in conversation with the following quote, from Colleen Lye's *America's Asia: Racial Form and American Literature, 1893–1945* (Princeton University Press, 2005): "To the extent that American universality depends upon the possibility of assimilation, there is always also the danger of discovering aliens in our midst, or the wholesale possibility of American takeover by aliens."

"Alien Miss Reads Section 14" is a poem written after reading the transcripts of the Chinese Exclusion Acts, which barred Chinese immigrants from entering the country in 1882—not unlike Donald Trump's 2017 proposed Muslim ban. The questions outlined in this poem ("*how many stairs . . . gold tooth?*") are adapted from examination text given to "paper sons and daughters," Chinese immigrants who were the "children" of Chinese American citizens on paper (sourced from R. D. McKenzie's *Oriental Exclusion* [University of Chicago Press, 1928]). I am indebted to Sophie Stid, who helped me find the place of this poem within the "Alien Miss" series.

"Alien Miss at the Immigration Station" refers to the Chinese immigrants detained in the Angel Island Immigration Station barracks. In 1970, poetry (written in Chinese calligraphy) was discovered at the station, etched into the walls. "*Don't fall for all this Western façade / Even if it is jade filled, it is still a cage*" was one such discovered line. I recommend Judy Yung's essay "A

Bowlful of Tears: Chinese Women Immigrants on Angel Island" in *Frontiers* for supplemental reading. The text in section 2 is sourced directly from the Chinese Exclusion Act, passed in 1882 (via the Avalon Project at Yale Law School). The speaker in this poem is based on my own imagination and my research.

"Alien Miss Consults Her Past" takes its italicized text from an 1885 broadside letter, "To the president of the United States, and to the Senate and House of Representatives in Congress assembled [Protest against ill-treatment of the Chinese. s. l., 1885]," now archived at the Library of Congress.

"Alien Miss Confronts the Author" takes its italicized texts from several sources: the California Parks & Recreation "Angel Island State Park" website; the Chinese Exclusion Acts (1882) legal transcript; the History Channel website's "Chinese Exclusion Act" text; a self-transcribed email to the Museum of Chinese in America, written (with no response) to HR in June 2019. I am very grateful to the wonderful crew at Tin House, who generously provided me with time, space, and genuine support to create this sequence during a writing residency in the summer of 2019.

"'The Situation Is Gratifying'" is a persona poem, based on Chinese propaganda posters during the Cultural Revolution in mainland China. The particular propaganda poster that inspired this poem was designed by Yan Guiming in October 1974 and interested me for its performance of public allegiance and "gratitude." The speaker and other figures in this poem are fictional, yet much of the emotional core is based on conversations with men and women who grew up during the Cultural Revolution, my own research, and my poetic projection. Many thanks to Yaoyao Liu for providing invaluable historical knowledge that informed this poem.

"Poem for Clara Elizabeth Chan Lee" was inspired by a visit to the Museum of Chinese in America in New York. Clara Elizabeth Chan Lee was the first Chinese American woman to vote.

"Baba Encounters Knife and Fork" was written in conversation with Sun Wukong, the Monkey King. For additional reading and poetic imaginings of the Monkey King, I recommend (and am inspired by) Jasmine An's *Monkey Was Here* (Porkbelly Press, 2020). In this poem, as well as within other poems in the "Lineage Of" section, I drew from Rita Dove's words of wisdom, in her 1989 interview with Steven Schneider in the *Iowa Review*: "I was after the essence of my grandparents' existence and their survival, not necessarily the facts of their survival. . . . One appropriates certain gestures from the factual life to reinforce a larger sense of truth that is not, strictly speaking, reality."

Section v of "I Make a New Song for Myself" was written amid the COVID-19 pandemic, in response to the following exchange between an Al Jazeera reporter and Donald Trump in March 2020: "'And do you think, using the term "Chinese virus," that puts Asian-Americans at risk, that people might target them?' A reporter asked at the news conference. 'No, not at all,' Trump reiterated. 'I think they probably would agree with it 100 percent. It comes from China.'"

"Wài Gōng Is Dancing" is in memory of my grandfather and adapts a line from the Derek Walcott poem "Love after Love."

"Sitting on a U.S. Bench, a Mosquito Takes My Blood" was written in response to the Department of Homeland Security's (quiet) announcement, in 2017, that it would begin monitoring social media accounts and internet search histories of legalized and naturalized U.S. citizens, updating the "A-file," or Alien File, of the official record-keeping system for immigrants undergoing the citizenship process.

The title "The Thematics of Blood" is modified from a line in Ann Stoler's *Race and the Education of Desire* (Duke University Press, 2005). The image is sourced from a personal screenshot of Google Search on February 17, 2018.

"Possible" references Sally Rooney's novel *Normal People* (Hogarth, 2018).

"Attending Compline Service as a Nonbeliever" was inspired by conversation and guidance from the brilliant Molly Williams.

"Vision while Running on the Vanderbilt Indoor Track" pays homage to a chorus of women, including my grandmother; Clara Elizabeth Chan Lee; and the late Taiwanese singer Teresa Teng and her song "**月亮代表我的心**" (The Room Represents My Heart).

"Say a Little Prayer" was a poem born after reading about Nüshu, "Women's writing," a system of writing created and used exclusively by women in the Hunan province of southern China—an extinct language, as the last known speaker died in 2004. I love the idea of women who created a language exclusively for themselves—writing their bodies and their linkages into being.

WISCONSIN POETRY SERIES

Edited by Ronald Wallace and Sean Bishop

(B) = Winner of the Brittingham Prize in Poetry
(FP) = Winner of the Felix Pollak Prize in Poetry
(4L) = Winner of the Four Lakes Prize in Poetry

Fruit (4L) • Bruce Snider

The Year We Studied Women (FP) • Bruce Snider

Bird Skin Coat (B) • Angela Sorby

The Sleeve Waves (FP) • Angela Sorby

If the House (B) • Molly Spencer

Wait (B) • Alison Stine

Hive (B) • Christina Stoddard

The Red Virgin: A Poem of Simone Weil (B) • Stephanie Strickland

The Room Where I Was Born (B) • Brian Teare

Fragments in Us: Recent and Earlier Poems (FP) • Dennis Trudell

The Apollonia Poems (4L) • Judith Vollmer

Level Green (B) • Judith Vollmer

Reactor • Judith Vollmer

Voodoo Inverso (FP) • Mark Wagenaar

Hot Popsicles • Charles Harper Webb

Liver (FP) • Charles Harper Webb

The Blue Hour (B) • Jennifer Whitaker

Centaur (B) • Greg Wrenn

Pocket Sundial (B) • Lisa Zeidner